# 797,885 Books

are available to read at

# Forgotten Books

## www.ForgottenBooks.com

Forgotten Books' App
Available for mobile, tablet & eReader

ISBN 978-1-330-59548-0
PIBN 10066928

This book is a reproduction of an important historical work. Forgotten Books uses state-of-the-art technology to digitally reconstruct the work, preserving the original format whilst repairing imperfections present in the aged copy. In rare cases, an imperfection in the original, such as a blemish or missing page, may be replicated in our edition. We do, however, repair the vast majority of imperfections successfully; any imperfections that remain are intentionally left to preserve the state of such historical works.

Forgotten Books is a registered trademark of FB &c Ltd.
Copyright © 2017 FB &c Ltd.
FB &c Ltd, Dalton House, 60 Windsor Avenue, London, SW19 2RR.
Company number 08720141. Registered in England and Wales.

For support please visit www.forgottenbooks.com

# 1 MONTH OF FREE READING

at

www.ForgottenBooks.com

By purchasing this book you are eligible for one month membership to ForgottenBooks.com, giving you unlimited access to our entire collection of over 700,000 titles via our web site and mobile apps.

To claim your free month visit:

www.forgottenbooks.com/free66928

\* Offer is valid for 45 days from date of purchase. Terms and conditions apply.

English
Français
Deutsche
Italiano
Español
Português

# www.forgottenbooks.com

**Mythology** Photography **Fiction**
Fishing Christianity **Art** Cooking
Essays Buddhism Freemasonry
Medicine **Biology** Music **Ancient Egypt** Evolution Carpentry Physics
Dance Geology **Mathematics** Fitness
Shakespeare **Folklore** Yoga Marketing
**Confidence** Immortality Biographies
Poetry **Psychology** Witchcraft
Electronics Chemistry History **Law**
Accounting **Philosophy** Anthropology
Alchemy Drama Quantum Mechanics
Atheism Sexual Health **Ancient History**
**Entrepreneurship** Languages Sport
Paleontology Needlework Islam
**Metaphysics** Investment Archaeology
Parenting Statistics Criminology
**Motivational**

# The Modern Deity

BY

THOMAS WALKER MALCOLM
PASTOR OF ST. ANDREW'S PRESBYTERIAN CHURCH
DETROIT, MICHIGAN

---

INTRODUCTION BY
JAMES MORRISON BARKLEY, D. D.
FORMER MODERATOR OF THE GENERAL ASSEM-
BLY OF THE PRESBYTERIAN CHURCH
IN THE U. S. A.

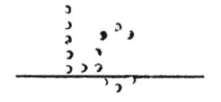

THE GRISWOLD PRESS
DETROIT

BR 525
.M25

COPYRIGHT, 1911, BY T. W. MALCOLM

TO

### The Memory of My Father and Mother

*Who early taught me the value of living "not by
bread alone but by every word that
proceedeth out of the mouth
of God,"
I dedicate this little volume
In sorrowful and affectionate remembrance
of their love and virtues.*

# PREFATORY NOTE.

This little volume is a study of the Moral, Religious and Sociological conditions of our age. It is an attempt to show the trend of the times, and to offer an antidote. There is no effort at literary finish; simply an earnest, sober and unprejudiced setting forth of the causes of the fretted life of to-day. It is published in response to urgent requests with the hope that it may serve the purpose for which it was intended, namely, to persuade us that

"We are not here to play, to dream, to drift.
We have hard work to do, and loads to lift.
Shun not the struggle; face it, 'tis God's gift—
BE STRONG.

T. W. M.

# INTRODUCTION.

My friend, Mr. Malcolm, has struck a theme that cries for treatment. Modern Baalism is no more moral or modest or merciful than its ancient prototype of the days of Ahab and Jezebel. It needs now, as it needed then, rough handling. And the writer whose pages follow, has turned loose upon it a vehement and torrential earnestness of denunciation. The stream of his ideas and the rush of his convictions are so strong and swift that they cannot "purl along in the ditched out channel of conventional phrase." They overflow the banks. They cut their own channel. At times, they toss aside the elegance, and even the accuracy, of style to rush right on to the author's objective. Yet the work is not devoid of style. In places it is truly eloquent; and it is enriched by choice and copious quotations. In temper, it is strongly and sanely optimistic. Discrediting the dread evils that fret our times, it rises to positiveness in pointing the pathway of relief in a return to righteousness and soberness and truth.

I commend it to the sympathetic perusal and practice of all who would follow an earnest mind on a great theme.

JAMES MORRISON BARKLEY.

# The Modern Deity.

QUARANTANIA, or as it is called in Arabic, Kuruntul, a mountainous region in the far east, between Jerusalem and Jericho, is not so familiar a word as Gettysburg or Waterloo. Historians never record it among the names of the world's great battlefields. Yet, battlefield it was. And if we reckon the fierceness of the conflict, the issues at stake, and the beneficent results accruing, we must give it a large and conspicuous place in our thought. The name, however, is traditional, but the battle is fact. It was bloodless, to be sure. Great conquests are always so. Not armies drawn up with "reeking tube and iron shard." Just two contestants. Two men? Yes, and no. A Man and an angel—a fallen angel. Yea, the Prince of Peace and the Prince of Devils. Though bloodless, it was not weaponless. A word is often mightier than a sword. This is absolutely so when it is the Word of God. Keener than a two-edged Damascus blade was the instrument by which the enemy was utterly vanquished. What a terrific and decisive thrust: "It is written, man shall not live by bread alone, but by every word that proceedeth out of the mouth of God."

"It is written." Where? In Deuteronomy eighth chapter third verse; the second giving of the law; the recapitulation of man's experience in his relationship with God. It was the Divine word that came to Israel through Moses, and in which the Son of God in His wilderness temptation made answer to Satan's suggestion, that He put His material wants first. If He were the Messiah why should He go hungry? Why not thrust aside all such weak, fleshly conditions by His power? The idea of the King of Israel suffering from hunger! It was out of harmony with the character of the exalted Sovereign. It tended to degrade Him; to belittle Him before the eyes of men; to dethrone His real nobility! "If thou be the Son of God, command that these stones be made bread." "But He answered, It is written, Man shall not live by bread alone, but by every word that proceedeth out of the mouth of God."

By this quotation He would remind the tempter of the fact, that the performing of the proposed miracle was a very small matter, as such. Had not God been performing daily, for forty years,

## THE MODERN DEITY.

a miracle, by which He had provided enough bread for two and a half millions of people; and had He not in proof of the fact that He and the Father were one, provided enough to feed several thousand people with five loaves and two small fishes, and gathered up twelve baskets' full of the fragments that remained? The proposed miracle was a small matter, but what God had been doing for others, He refused to do for Himself, and scorned to do at the suggestion of the devil, and gives the best of reasons, when He says, "Man shall not live by bread alone." And even satan was convinced that this was true, for he was foiled by the Divine logic, and surely, such convincing truth is worthy of reverent and receptive consideration.

There are few among us who do not like to be regarded as optimists, and our most dreaded enemy is he who calls us pessimistic. If by optimism we mean a culturing of ourselves to the adoption of that attitude which declines to see the dark, disagreeable and unpleasant facts of life; an optimism after the flabby, jelly-fish type; a namby-pambyism that ostrich-like buries its head in the sand and refuses to look squarely in the face of things as they are. If that is the optimism we covet and by which we wish to be known, then I must be counted out of the company. It isn't enough, however, to look on the bright side—better have a look at both sides. And in doing so, one need not succumb to a case of hypochondria, nor become so blinded as to suppose there is more pain than pleasure; more tears than laughter; that the groans of earth far exceeds its glories, and to be so profoundly overwhelmed by the seriousness of life that it must be viewed through glasses of indigo, and

"Wear long faces, just as if our Maker,
The Lord of goodness, were an undertaker."

But can there be a cowardice more dishonorable than that which shows in itself a disinclination to see and face the darker facts which cloud so perceptibly the otherwise brighter aspects of life? And is he a lesser patriot who is willing to see these things, and seeing them, give to them a voice of articulate utterance? Or, rather, is it not treasonable to dope the torturing evils which afflict humanity with the soothing-syrup of "all is well," and thus turning our evidence in the case into perjury? Not a stooping to slander; nor to the babbling of idiotic foolishness, no, not that, but when a man gets sight of prevailing and thriving evils that must ever burn their deep significance into the consciousness of every honest citizen, then to seal the lips and fling down the pen, and to contemptably count the cost in the ridicule and scorn of those whose mock patriotism has led them to exalt the rule of silence to a pedestal of honor, is treason as dark and loathsome as that which turned the face of Benedict Arnold's picture to the wall. And we exclaim with Scotland's poet:

> "Wha will be a traitor knave?
> Wha can fill a coward's grave?"

And believing that the old Latin proverb rings true, "suppressio veri suggestio falsi," i. e., the suppression of the truth is the suggestion of a lie; one can readily see that it is not at all necessary to peer through blue spectacles to affirm without prejudice, that when it comes to a proposition such as Satan propounded most men will be found on the devil's side, and that many who would unhesitatingly reject the classification, will stand with him in his argument that "one must live." And this, too, in the face of the fact, that men know this truth which Christ here enunciated, but hate it with a satanic hatred; it jars

## THE MODERN DEITY.

upon their false conceptions, and gives a severe jolt to unworthy ambition. And why?

Because the body is everything. There is nothing of greater value than flesh and blood, and the wiseacres are right in reducing thought and feeling to those constituent elements. Man is but so many gallons of water, so many pounds of carbon, with smaller quantities of phosphorus, sulphur, potassium, iron and other substances, which you will see carefully sealed in jars on the shelves in the laboratory. Therefore, we are mere automata, as science would have us believe, clockwork machines wound up by meat and drink. Bread is everything. Bread is the thing in which we live and move and have our being. Provision stores are our temples and the keepers thereof our priests. The bodily life is the subject of all bliss. Bread is the foundation. Take away bread and bliss departs, man dies, and there is the end to it. The necessary conditions for happiness are in the digestive organs.

> "'Live while you live,' the epicure will say,
> 'And seize the pleasures of the present day.'"

# THE MODERN DEITY.

## An Idolatrous Age.

That the times are out of tune needs scarcely to be said. It may be true that whenever wise men have taken to thinking about their times, they have always thought evil of them. But the fact of the matter is, the times have gone wrong before the wise men take to the business of thinking about them at all. We are rarely conscious of our constitutions until they trouble us by disorder. "Thou shalt have no other gods before Me." Thus the decalogue opens. That decalogue has never been annulled. In the presence of the one living and true God, let no other be presumed. Upon the proper recognition of that edict depends the happiness of individuals and the destiny of nations. It has always been so; it is so now. But what's the use to argue the existence of God? True, to argue that there is a God is as wise as to argue that there is a sun, but the blind see not the sun, the blind see not God. Eyes have they, but they see not. Ears have they, but they hear not. There is a god, however, which men do see. It needs no argument to prove his existence. A god so real, so omniptent, so omnipresent that it seems well nigh futile to attempt to argue the existence of any other. It is neither Venus nor Bacchus, but it is Plutus. There is no doubt about it. Plutus, in one or other of its forms, is the man-created deity, to which large numbers are bowing down with a blindness only equaled by their devotion.

The mention of idolatry turns the thoughts of most men to the poor, half-naked, half-starved heathen with the altar of their god at the door. But we need not go so far afield. Let us come home, sit down and take a good square look at ourselves. Worse than that of ancient days is the paganism of these opening years of the twentieth century. A paganism in the throes of incessant revival. And I am bold to suggest that while people's eyes are too blind to perceive the God of Heaven, and their ears too dull to hear the voice of the Infinite, they are ever ready to behold the shining face of this American dollar which I hold before you and to listen to its metallic voice. I point to this dollar and say, "These be thy gods." While traveling in Europe the writer remarked, with what he felt a just pride, to a fellow passenger, that he was from the United States, at which the Londoner turned upon him with "That's where the dollar is Al-

## THE MODERN DEITY.

mighty?" Well, whether we like it or not, and I confess it was not to my liking, that is how others see us. When South Sea Islanders are turning from cannibal feasts to sacraments, and heathen nations bending before the eternal God, all this is in strange contrast to the heathenism in Christian lands where paganism seems to have its loudest voice, until we are having it prophesied that the now so-called heathen world may one day raise the heaven-inspired battle-cry, "The Western World for Christ," and with Crusades carrying the enlightening Gospel, seek to bring us back to a lost faith.

> "Do not I love thee, god of gold?
> Inspect my soul and see.
> In dungeon deep, and dark, and cold,
> Lies conscience slain for thee."

## An American Disease.

It is said, that America has the distinction of contributing a number of diseases to the long list of ailments that afflict the human family—diseases which even the Old World is largely unfamiliar with. Appendicitis is said to be one of these. Up to twenty years ago it was not prevalent in Europe, although occasional cases did occur. In a lecture reported to have been delivered at St. Thomas' Hospital, London, William Henry Battle, F. R. C. S., declared his belief that the spread of appendicitis was due to the world-wide use of American foodstuffs. Let that be as it may, there is a moral disease that is prevalent in its acutest forms in America, namely, Materialism, whose symptoms are money-madness and pleasure-madness. And the cause has been given in the intellectual and moral food upon which the age is made to feed.

In an age which boasts that it can scratch the Lord's Prayer on one side of a ten-cent piece and the Ten Commandments on the other side; when morals are reduced to vulgar fractions; when the chief subject in the curriculum of life is that ten cents make a dime and ten dimes make a dollar, you, my reader, will agree with me in this, at least, that the god of materialism is better known, vastly more popular, and more faithfully loved than the God of Heaven in whose hands our very breath is, and who in mercy permits an age of such unequaled prosperity. We read what a journalist is reported to have asserted that "The last century opened with three million Americans who loved liberty, and closed with seventy-five millions who loved money," and we are exceedingly anxious to modify that statement by adding that it was said "sweepingly." But we need not pierce to any depth the crust of society in order to discover that there is a vast amount of truth in the satirical fling.

There is no kind of atheism so prevalent and so formidable today as Materialism. A materialism that, with the most insolent mien brazenly asserts, that prosperity is the only heaven, and adversity the only hell. That to "get on" is the acme of human happiness, and to "succeed" is the final goal of life. That big "I" is the one whose urgent claims we must heed, and the only tribunal to which we must render account. That the first personal pronoun is the base from which all else must be considered; the center from which

## THE MODERN DEITY.

all must emanate; the pivot around which all must revolve. Let me quote from another—four lines which constitute the whole of a poem. It fits to a nicety the modern philosophy of life:

"I, I, I, I itself I;
The inside and outside, the what and the why;
The when and the where, the low and the high;
All I, I, I, I itself I."

They certainly sound like a take-off on some hide-bound egotist, or else the babble of a comic poet. But they are neither. They are rather the motto of a pagan religion in our time, called "Christian Science," embodying as they do, the essence of the entire system. It well defines the source from which flows the paganism embodied in our theme, but swinging to quiet the other extreme, however, in its practical development. A form of idolatry as dark and degrading as that of the most benighted heathen who bows down to wood and stone. Of course we will at once repudiate the charge, and in burning fervor exclaim, "I am no idolater." But not so fast. The thing a man thinks most of, that is his god. Money is worshiped just as truly as if silver dollars were piled up before men and they prayed

## THE MODERN DEITY.

to them every day. It is not all necessary to have a gilded image, but the age talks more about money, thinks more about money, and prays more about money than any preceding generation in the world's history. Nor does it depend upon the size of the idol. The rich are not its only devotees. In non-Christian lands, there are idols of mammoth dimensions, but there are also many that are very small, so small they might be set in an earring. But idols all. May it not be said in truth, that it is the man who has little or no money who most frequents the shrine? The idolatry of the poor man is as pagan as the one who has secured it by the same devotion. The differentiating feature being merely the size of the idol. One grasps dollars, the other pennies, but both grasp.

> "To live for self, to think of self,
> For self and none beside."

It has crept into our universities, offering its tempting "foundations" to boards of trustees and faculties, who prostrate before those who can furnish endowments, and leading youth to turn away from the wealth of mentality as of less value than that of business, by which to attain one's bread and butter and roof. One may pick up the commencement addresses of many leading institutions of "higher" learning and find inspiration for all of life's pursuits, but with scarcely the slightest hint concerning man's higher interests, interests which must put all other pursuits into eternal shade, until from the lips of one, who by reason of his illustrious father, sets a pace, and who had won honors for scholarship, we hear this: "That is nothing, I had much rather be good at baseball and football." And what shall we say of gifted men, men in possession of choice literary gifts, who might win renown, yet wasting them as a prodigal wastes his strength on foolish and worthless things.

## Present Day Materialism.

What then, in a word, is the definition of Materialism? It is the deification of matter. Matter is eternal. Matter is God. It asserts that there is no separate spiritual substance. That man is earth-born, earth-bound and earth-destined. That sin lies in the material and not in the will to do evil. That all things take place under a law, which is called the law of "necessity." That the true philosophy of life is the "philosophy of dirt." A noted writer puts into the mouth of one of his heroes the question, "What do you believe?" And the reply is, "I believe in that," stamping his foot on the ground. What a sorry world, when men assume that perception by the senses is the only basis of belief; when man will believe only in that which is seen and tangible! When the realities of an inner world of consciousness is degraded to a level with the brute. A materialism continually urging the legitimatcy of our struggle for bread and clothes and shelter and things, until the conflict to secure these obscures the ultimate reason for their use. And after all, wherein lies the value of these things, save as they make us men and women who live to make life for others a better, purer and more perfect life? Whenever any other motive of human progress has superseded that, progress has ceased, disintegration has set in, whether in men or nations.

W. H. Mallock, in "The New Republic," gives a terrible arraignment of the blind materialism of our time, which he puts into the mouth of Mr. Herbert: "The age is now wandering in an accursed wilderness which not only shows no hill-tops whence the promised land may be seen, but which to most of the wanderers seems a promised land itself. And they have a God of their own, too, who engages now to lead them out of it if they will follow him who, for visible token of the godhead, leads them with a pillar of cloud by day and a pillar of fire by night, the cloud being the black smoke of their factory chimneys and the fire the red glare of their blast furnaces. And so effectual are these modern divine guides that if we were standing on the brink of Jordan itself we should be utterly unable to catch, through the fire and the smoke, one single glimpse of the sunset hills beyond." This is a picture of the materialism of our day. Is it too vivid? What is it but the absorption of men in material pursuits that is the cause of such widespread disregard and neglect of the obligations we have to Almighty God. So deeply are men immersed in the getting and the having end of life that there is no other interest which gives them concern. The Hindus have a festival at which they pay divine honors to the implements of their trades. The blacksmith brings his hammer, the carpenter his saw, the farmer his plow; and they bow down and worship them. We have a revival of that paganism here in America in the absorbing devotion of life's pursuits; the mortgaging of every energy to the getting of a livelihood to the neglect of our real life. A form of idolatry so base, so terrible in its power, so cruel to its victims, so cancer-like in its consumption of the soul's capacity for happiness, and so sure and speedy is the Nemesis that pursues indulgence therein, that anyone with his eye upon the drifts of the times could well say in the words of Hamlet:

> "*  *  * But that I am forbid
> To tell the secrets of this prison-house,
> I could a tale unfold, whose lightest word
> Would harrow up your soul."

We may deny all this in our sober thought and seek to refute these tenets of our materialistic times, but that in no way explodes the fact, that such is the living creed of the masses. We may say that we believe in an all-intelligent, all-wise and an all-loving God, inscribe it on our coin and sing it in our anthem, yet the mass of men are living as if there were no such God at all.

We see this in its practical development in several ways:

# THE MODERN DEITY.

## The Craze of Commerce.

The ideal man is the one who turns everything into gold; the man who gets and holds and then goes on to get more and hold more. Agassiz' wise reply to the lecture bureau—"I have no time to make money"—sounds like a bit of insanity. Gordon's refusal to accept reward from the Chinese Emperor for his services in the Tai Ping rebellion, and who on his arrival in England, declined every honor, preferring to bury himself in obscurity, and the very medals that were showered upon him he put no value upon, and would even have them melted down to provide relief to the poor, sounds like a piece of Quixotism. Luther's refusal to accept a considerable sum of money sent to him, and when he prayed that night, "Lord, Thou must not think to put me off with a portion like that; I want Thyself," seems nothing short of foolishness. "The simple life" as lived by Thoreau in the wilderness, and as pictured by Wagner, appears to us only an idyllic dream. The suggestion of Paul, "Having food and raiment we have enough," is ridiculed as antiquated. Our feeling today scorns all such

## THE MODERN DEITY.

moderation. To make a living is not enough; to secure comfort for self and family is considered an exceedingly small thing; but to toil and struggle for dazzling prizes—the success that glitters—that is the one thing. It is said that a minister walking on the street of a certain city overheard the talk of some university students. Looking upon the gleaming equipages and splendid silks flitting by, one said: "I tell you, boys, it is money that goes in this town." And the belief that it is money that goes is the evidence of a well nigh universal sentiment. The services of man without an itch for reward, the quiet, unostentatious sacrifice of personal gain or personal interest for the good of others, these have all but died out, and if not altogether passed away, are repudiated as sheer folly. The mad race of the ignoble crowd for wealth draws like the suction of a maelstrom, or entices like the song of the siren, until dazed and dizzied by the fierce momentum, men forget all else and are transformed into mere money-makers, offering this achievement to the soul as the standard of life.

The Saturday Evening Post tells the story of the president of the Yellowstone Park Association, who traveled in Europe, having for a companion a man interested in the hotel business.

# THE MODERN DEITY.

After they had traveled over Europe, investigating hotel and commissary problems, they finally arrived in Rome. They went to St. Peter's and stood beneath the dome. "Well," said the park president, "here it is; here's the dome." The hotel man took a look upward. Then turning to the speaker, said, "How much did that man in London say he wanted for them hams?" *"Them hams"* had blinded him to the awe-inspiring wonders of the cathedral, annihilating everything else. And this subordinating man to his material interests, sinks his life in them, foregoes mental culture, moral elevation, spiritual activity and all that goes to make a complete manhood; quenches all lofty aspirations, gets, gathers and holds all things, enthrones himself on and among them, lets every faculty be so concentrated so that the faculty for getting and getting-on grows strongest. This, this is the godless commercialism we find measuring success by the standard of the market-place; the sinking of other and worthier aims in the eager rush for gain. It makes synonymous terms of dollars and dominion. Wisdom is exchanged for wealth, loyalty for loot and God for gain. Homes are exchanged for harems, daughters for dirt and purity for position. Love, patriotism and honesty, the triple graces which make a nation strong, have their prices fixed.

"Oh, cursed love of gold; when for thy sake
The fool throws up his interest in both worlds;
First starved in this, then damn'd in that to come."

THE MODERN DEITY.

## The Controlling Principle.

When Pope Pius IV. heard of the death of John Calvin he declared that that "heretic's" strength lay in this, that money never had the slightest charm for him. If therein lay Calvin's strength, surely the spell which money throws over a man shows his weakness. Ruskin said: "Money-making is an all-absorbing game, and we knock each other down oftener in playing at that than at football or any rougher sport." "Business is business" is the controlling motto under this blind despotism. Editors will publish not what the people essentially need, but want. If the readers want the editorial page abbreviated or cut out and the sporting pages increased, then "business is business," and presto, it is done. Under the dominion of the dollar the world is filled with books that "sell" and not especially with books that elevate. To please if not to amuse a flippant public, writers trim their sails to catch the breeze of popular favor. Five novels of various complexions are born into the world each day, according to somebody's reckoning. One of our foremost writers has told how his more serious books on vital topics brought him little or no return, whereas for his little effort in turning out novels and magazine articles of a light and airy nature, he secured the greatest recognition and profit. And to accept coronation at the hands of the fickle public, rather than a conscience void of offense, is the temptation which few writers can resist; for the public wants nothing so much as to be amused. The cheapest doggerel must crush out the finest heart-hymns, and "Home, Sweet Home," "Jesus, Lover of My Soul," and the like, have their melody strangled with "ragtime," the thinnest skim-milk which today wears the dignity of music, till music walks with shamed face in a land where patriots were made, largely because they were thrilled with the lofty songs of the church and fireside. Indeed, it has tainted the very centers of citizenship. A Canadian judge in the court of general sessions recently created a sensation by refusing applications for naturalization papers. "Many of these people," said the judge, "come here and ask for naturalization papers, though they never intend to become citizens. They simply use the certificates for commercial purposes.

## THE MODERN DEITY.

A man to whom we granted such papers sometime ago, came to the clerk and asked for another certificate, because the one we gave him was worn out. No doubt he had loaned it to others for a like use, at so many dollars. The clerk was not even sure it was the same man to whom the certificate had originally been granted." And we are tempted to cry out that "man's chief end is to glorify gold and to enjoy it forever."

But more, the passion for pelf hesitates not to leap to the very summit of its avariciousness, and demands that which is more precious than life, for fuel to feed its ever glowing fire, until trafficking in white slavery is not only no longer a concealed fact in so far as it concerns those directly involved, but is open and wholesale under the finest names of legitimate business. There must be a hell deep and dark for the buyers and sellers in the trade, but is there no such place for the consciousless corporation, which pays a girl the starvation wage of $3.50 per week, and who must sell out her virtue (not from choice but necessity) in order to live? Which will you say is the guiltier—the brute who buys the product on the street, or the heartless demons who have manufactured it by their greed?

## THE MODERN DEITY.

"Gold! Gold! Gold! Gold!
Bright and yellow, hard and cold,
Molten, graven, hammered and rolled;
Heavy to get and light to hold;
Hoarded, bartered, bought and sold,
Stolen, borrowed, squandered, doled;
Spurned by the young, but hugged by the old
To the very verge of the churchyard mold;
Price of many a crime untold;
Gold! gold! gold! gold!
Good or bad a thousandfold;
   How widely its agencies vary—
To save—to ruin—to curse—to bless—
As even its minted coins express
Now stamped with the image of good Queen Bess,
   And now of a Bloody Mary."

"What is he worth?" we ask concerning the rich man, when we should inquire "What did it cost him?" Prosperity may be poverty, or, as Ruskin put it, "Wealth may be illth." Conceive of a harp selling its strings to buy music; parting with them one by one, beginning with the bass, until at last it finds its power to make music wholly gone. In a similar way men are bartering soul wealth for body gain, pawning the jewels of

## THE MODERN DEITY.

their immortality for the treasures of time, only to discover in the end that a rich soul is always rich and all are poor beside.

The current phrases of our day are fearful witnesses of its rank atheism: e. g., "My company will be the loser by $25,000 if this fanatical scheme goes through." "Fools will be fools, anyway, and we might just as well profit by their foolishness as some other concern." "One man's money is as good as another's, and who cares how he drops it so long as it reaches our till in the end." "What the people want they will get, and we might as well have their trade as another." "We all love the teachings of the Master, but this is a business proposition pure and simple," and so on ad infinitum. Up to the neck in bills and accounts and invoices and orders, they have not a corner in their heart, or of their time, for matters religious. The stock market is more important. "Money stringent." "Wheat weaker." "Cotton steady." "Steel depressed." "Flour; buyers more free," and so forth. This is a specimen of the language of commerce, which tells how intently men are on the mad race for earthly things.

And how surprising to hear men, of whom better might be expected, conniving at dishonor-

## THE MODERN DEITY.

able practices or petty frauds, on the grounds that they are necessary, or universal. "You must just wink at a good deal at what you cannot approve." "It is impossible to get on in this city if you are too strait-laced." And so, conscience, like a drugged watch-dog, makes but feeble remonstrance. What a condescension to such a standard of morality! If this be the accepted commercial custom, rendered necessary, and hence innocent by its universality, then sin needs only to be widespread to transform it into a virtue. Arthur Clough has put it in his "Latest Decalog":

> "Thou shalt have one God only; who
> Would be at the expense of two?
> No graven image may be
> Worshiped save in the currency.
> Swear not at all, since for thy curse
> Thine enemy is none the worse.
> At church on Sunday to attend
> Will serve to keep the world thy friend.
> Honor thy parents; that is all
> By whom advancement may befall.
> Thou shalt not kill, but needst not strive
> Officiously to keep alive.
> Adultery is not fit

## THE MODERN DEITY.

Or safe for woman to commit.
Thou shalt not steal; an empty feat
When 'tis more lucrative to cheat.
Bear not false witness; let the lie
Have time on its own·wings to fly.
Thou shalt not covet; but tradition
Approves all forms of competition."

The man who puts gold above God, chattels above character, and mammon above manhood, has inverted God's order and is surely and swiftly paving his downward way. He was not far wrong who said: "The only crosses some people bear are gold ones." And when we are told that in a certain manufacturing city in England bronze idols are made in thousands for the Hindoos, by men who every Sunday pray for their conversion, we are tempted to believe that the poet struck a keynote in saying 'tradition approves all forms of competition,' and reveals the baseness to which a godless commercialism reduces men; a baseness which is kin to martyrdom—a martyrdom of conscience and the first principles of integrity. In the times of the Romish Inquisition there was a horrible form of punishment for heretics, called "The Virgin's Kiss." The victim was pushed forward to kiss an image of the Virgin, when, lo, its arms immediately enclosed him in a deadly embrace, piercing his body with a hundred hidden spikes. Many a man has found personal gratification to be like that beautiful and seemingly harmless figure. And yielding to its solicitation is only to be "pierced through with many sorrows." Or like the little boy who for months had been gathering up prune-stones, being fond of the kernel, and wishing to prepare for himself a great treat, laid up a considerable store. At last came the day of anticipated enjoyment; he ate them all, and after hours of intense agony, died. And men who have concentrated all their energies upon amassing money, preparing a veritable banquet of enjoyment for the evening-time of life, have sat down to the sumptuously prepared feast, when, lo, death sits at the table, too. Or like the Italian nobleman who took this terrible revenge on one whom he hated. He set him alive in a niche in the palace he was building and piled row upon row of bricks and stones about him, until the wall closed over him, and shut him in his dark and awful tomb. We shrink in horror at such a tale, but it is a symbol of what many men are constantly doing with their better selves—piling brick and stones about them, walling them in and leaving them there to die—

only the material is called by a different name. Many have buried their manhood in their business. In the inner chamber of many an otherwise beautiful life, hidden away from sight, is the grave of a human soul, a grave dug with a spade called greed. Hidden in many a beautiful garden of flowers is the sepulcher in which honor, purity, truth and virtue lie buried.

"It is not the fact that you're dead that counts,
It's only, HOW DID YOU DIE?"

One of the memorable places of interest to the tourist is Abbotsford. Beautiful for situation is that splendid pile overlooking the River Tweed with the Eildon Hills beyond. But one cannot ramble among the haunts of the poet without recalling a singular pathos connected with it. Sir Walter Scott, deceived by the architect's plans, was virtually ruined in building it. The counting of the cost was but to discover himself a hopeless debtor for a hundred thousand pounds. But listen to him: "What shall I do?" he said. "By God's grace, though I die penniless, I will cancel my obligations." And he did. In the terms of the money market, we say that a fortune makes a man, and that the loss of a fortune ruins him. What a miserable, petty and sordid standard of measurement! A fortune cannot make a man, nor can its loss prove his ruin.

> "It's no in titles nor in rank,
> It's no in wealth in Lun'on Bank
> To purchase peace and rest;
> It's no in makin' muehle mair,
> It's no in books, it's no in lear,
> To mak' us truly blest."

And when we consider the fountain-head whence streams the turbulent currents of jealousy and strife between nations, we shall find it in the fact that they are weighed simply as commercial assets. Not humanitarianism; not the desire to uplift the peoples have taken the powers of America and Europe into Asia and Africa— these are merely "by-products" of commerce. No, not these. But trade, pure and simple. Our prophetic eye, relative to the destiny of nations, sees their rise or fall through our commercial telescope which sweeps the horizon of their material needs, and the quantity of goods they buy or refuse to buy from us, decides their fate.

THE MODERN DEITY.

## The Discoveries of Science.

In this we have surpassed every other preceding age. Hidden mysteries have been brought to light. Forces hitherto unknown have yielded to our touch, until men are virtually drunk with its scientific triumphs. In order to illustrate the tremendous speed with which we move, we compare the snail-pace of the ox-cart with the flash of lightning. The world moves with an ever-increasing velocity. The machinery of life is so highly geared, and the momentum of things so intense, that, as Mr. Roosevelt has said, "it may break down." When the express train is clipping off the sixty or seventy odd miles an hour, look out for the axle! As one has observed, "Today a man can live the 969 years of Methuselah's life in ten years." But there may be more of the bane than the blessing in such a comparison. Did not the civilizations that flourished along the Mediterranean ages ago have much that might profitably be compared with our modern life, and we know that their wide material conquests, their mastery of mechanical appliances, their wealth and luxury, were but the sirenic prelude

## THE MODERN DEITY.

of their downfall. Marvelous material triumphs are no immunity to disaster. Like those ages, only to an alarmingly increased degree, we are less concerned with the manufacture of manhood than the conquest of nature. Girdling continents, compassing seas, conquering the air, and laying all things tributary to man's temporal gratification—in which there is much reason to rejoice—yet what a price to pay, when triumphant science lies down upon its own achievements to worship the creation rather than its Creator! And forgetful of the fact that

>"Back of the loaf is the snowy flour,
>And back of the flour, the mill;
>And back of the mill are the wheat and the shower,
>And the sun and the Father's will."

When we see the scientist measuring the distance of the stars; weighing the sun as in a balance; analyzing the chemical elements of remote orbs; predicting to a second the eclipses of the heavenly bodies; photographing far-off worlds, and reporting the results of his researches to a brother philosopher across the seas by means of a single wire, indeed, without even a wire, we stand back in dumb wonder before the achievements of the human mind, and ready to exclaim:

## THE MODERN DEITY.

"Man!
Thou pendulum 'twixt Deity and dust."

But has the age much to be really thankful for even in the face of all its marvels? It is true that all conditions of life are ameliorated, mind is daily pursuing farther its conquests over matter; and it is undoubtedly true that, other things being equal, the generation that travels sixty or seventy miles an hour is five or six times as civilized as the generation that travels only ten or twelve. But the fact is, the other things are not equal. Can we honestly say that an age which holds it a greater achievement to identify men with monkeys than to separate right from wrong; that the beneficent discoveries that saves us from an hour's illness, but in turn gives us a lifetime of heart-sickness; that all that is really sacred in the life of man have been banished or buried by the very things which we boast of as our civilization; can we say that we have really advanced, in the proper meaning of that term, as much as we like to boast?

I am quite well aware of the fact that some will accuse me of doing society an injustice, and will point to the enlightened interest that is everywhere on the spread, the light of intellectual and

## THE MODERN DEITY.

scientific research that is gilding with its effulgent rays all the avenues of modern thought; that the era of a freer, truer and ever-widening and grander view of things, is dawning o'er the world. But will these fashionable opinions bear the acid test of fact? We admit that, as a rule, the age is vastly better informed, that it has fewer prejudices and infinitely more knowledge than a hundred years ago. But why look merely at the knowledge itself? We should measure the effects of knowledge. Knowledge puts speech on the tongue of the parrot, but we do not trust our children to his scholastic training. As a repository of facts our age stands, unquestionably, the highest. But you cannot test the health of a generation by looking over its examination papers in physical science. Nor can you measure the value of its acquisition of knowledge by looking over its copy-book. What are we doing with it? That is the vital question. What of it, if the goal be simply what Huxley said: "To reclaim a little more land, to add something to the extent of our possession."

# THE MODERN DEITY.

## The Progress of Civilization.

In a physical sense, is mankind developing a better type, a stronger and healthier race? Intellectually, have we a higher standard of intelligence and a more creative capacity than the generations past? Morally and spiritually, is the race on the ascendency? It is wise to ask these questions, for we must concede that they are vital. The triumphant tread of material progress has trampled all other things beneath it or driven all things before it, so much so, that it would seem to have reached the ultimate limit of advancement, and our material comforts have been so multiplied that we are tempted to think that we are in the dawn of the long-expected Golden Age. But has this fashionable conception, this conquest of material things tended to that higher and truer test of progress, the moral and spiritual elevation of the race? If we are insistent upon an affirmative reply, it must be in the most superficial sense, for the facts of history are all against it, and you will fail to find any evidence that the material development of the ages has fed or fostered either the physical, mental or spiritual development of men.

We still retain in memory the nursery legends of the giants of olden time. Men of such mammoth proportions who could cross a river at a single stride, and step from mountain-top to mountain-top with the utmost ease. A French writer, an academician by the name of M. Henrion, writing upon the subject many years ago, said that the human stature between the beginning of the race to the time of Christ, had deteriorated. He maintained that Adam was 124 feet in height, and that Eve was but slightly shorter. A rapid degeneration set in and the human stature continued to shrink till Noah reached only 27 feet, Abraham 20 feet, and Moses 13 feet, the process continuing down to the Christian era, when it was arrested at a standard of a little under six feet, which standard has been maintained to the present day. Well, we have grown older, and we trust wiser, and have laid aside these old-time though fascinating tales and refuse to believe that, with some exceptions, the human beings then were much bigger than we are now. Science and archaeology were wont to confirm the views of those ancient legends when fossilized bones were

## THE MODERN DEITY.

unearthed, which made even the giants mentioned in history but dwarfs and pigmies. But the rapid advance of science in modern times easily dissipated these dream-like notions, and one but needs to look at the Egyptian mummies, the sculptured figures, the stone coffins and the wooden caskets in the British Museum to conclude that the human stature was not, to any marked degree, materially different in size from that of our own age. True, the spies sent into Canaan returned with the report that in comparison with the men they saw there, the Israelites were but grasshoppers. But Caleb and Joshua did not so describe them, and I am willing to accept the testimony of courage, though it be in the minority, than that of cowardice, though it be in the majority.

But supposing that we have maintained in physical size the traditions of the race, that in no way goes to prove that we are developing a better, a stronger and a healthier people. Under ordinary conditions a man of gigantic stature possesses no more vitality than one of a much smaller size. Avoirdupois is not the test of health. A strong physique cannot be measured by its bulk than the worth of a book by its thickness. Therefore the health and strength of a race is not weighed by quantity, but by quality. If we accept this theory, and it is both logical and reasonable on its very face, then we must, if facts are worth anything at all, conclude that, as a race, we are deteriorating with an alarming rapidity. When the United States called for volunteers in 1861, to uphold the Union in the War of the Rebellion, 12 per cent of the applicants for enlistment were rejected, failing to pass the physical examination. Thirty-seven years later, when in 1898 the call was made for men in the liberation of Cuba in the war with Spain, 58.1-10ths per cent of the applicants were rejected as physically unfit. We may argue this upon the theory that the standard of physical excellence during the latter period was higher than that of '61, but let it be so, the percentage of young men who are physically degenerating is a frightful commentary on the deterioration of the race, and requires no further proof.

That the fuller blaze of twenty centuries of enlightenment has no doubt quickened intellectual activity, is easily seen in the making of many books, the founding of libraries, and the increased desire for liberal learning. But this is only a surface estimate at best. With all the accumulation of intellectual privileges, it must be noted by every unprejudiced student of history, that the ancients far excelled us in the creative faculty. The poetic genius of the early Hebrews and Greeks we have by no means even paralleled. Nor do we begin to match the creative power of the sculpture of that period. And as for Aristotle's, Demosthenes', Cicero's, Dante's, Plato's and Shakespeare's, all our modern progress in mental equipment does not give birth to their duplicates.

If this be true of the creative faculty of the intellect, it is still more evident that the progress of material civilization has not been conducive to the production of moral and spiritual gianthood. And
> "Unless above himself he can
> Erect himself, how poor a thing is man!"

Indeed, may it not be said, that the material has militated against the moral and spiritual, just as the good is constantly the enemy of the best? And when we consider that the good was intended to be the servant of the best, we need not think at all deeply to discover the cause of failure. Where are the Joshuas who would stay sun and moon to do battle against the enemies of God? The Nehemiahs who refuse to sidestep their mission of reconstruction and go down to the rabble on the plains of Ono? The Lu-

## THE MODERN DEITY.

thers who will hurl ink-bottles, or anything else for that matter, at real devils? The John Knoxs who will preach righteousness though it offend royalty, and whose prayers are mightier than armies? We are not growing to any perceptible degree such spiritual athletes. To dismiss the question upon the time-worn theory that their times called for such men, will in no satisfactory way account for their existence. If there ever was a time when the need for such a type of gianthood to asail existing evils and to set up a true standard of manhood, that time was no more then than now.

"God give us men. A time like this demands
  Strong minds, great hearts, true faith and ready hands.
Men whom the lust of office does not kill;
Men whom the spoils of office cannot buy;
Men who have honor, men who will not lie.
Men who can stand before a demagogue
And damn his treacherous flatteries without winking;
Tall men, sun crowned, who live above the fog,
In public duty and in private thinking.
For while the rabble, with their thumb worn creeds,
Their large profession, and their little deeds,
Mingle in selfish strife, lo, Freedom weeps,
Wrong rules the land, and waiting Justice sleeps."

## Matrimonial Commercialism.

That the sacred precinct of the home has not been spared the foul touch of our modern materialism, is the conviction of unprejudiced minds. To such gigantic proportions has this grown that we have become the laughing stock of neighboring nations. Abigail the beautiful, was not the last woman who has wedded a Nabal the abominable, for his fabulous wealth, and who was willing to risk everything that she might be a rich man's wife. Such marriages are little short of massacres; such weddings are more like funerals where cupid is led forth fascinated by the bigness of the dollar mark, at which, instead of Mendelssohn's Wedding March, the Dead March of Saul would be more appropriate. Two immortal lives are united that two farms may be joined, or two fortunes merged. And to find a name for the union it is called "a love match," when in truth they are neither heartmates nor helpmates. Such alliances have no right to the sacred name of matrimony. Reminding us of the girl, who was exceedingly proud of herself because she had composed a piece of poetry; and when asked to repeat it, she gave it thus:

> "I wish I was married,
> And very well too;
> With plenty of money
> And nothing to do."

Or like the daughter of the Scotch elder who, in reply to her father's remark "It is a solemn thing to get married, lassie," said "Yes, father, but it is a more solemner thing not to get married at all."

It would be ludicrous were it not so sad. And while it is true, that our women of the civilized world are not in the market for sale, it would be hard to prove to the poor slaves on the auction blocks of Africa, when there is so much evidence to the contrary. The list of foreign titles that have been bought with American gold, and the bartering of our heiresses for foreign puppets, is a long and sad one. Titles that are as worthless as a cracked nut without the kernel, a very extravagant form of "foreign exchange" in the sphere of economics, but a form of unholy commercialism as base as the most abject slavery; a selling of our girls for the paltry price of a name, until we are constrained to exclaim, "O Matrimony,

## THE MODERN DEITY.

what crimes are committed in thy holy name!" It goes without saying, that the angel of love more frequently abides in the cottage than in the palace, simply because love is not conditioned by the dimensions of a dwelling, nor by the standard of gold. These have never swayed the heart's affections, it demands a price far higher than that, a price that mere things cannot buy. And a heart subjected to a moneyed-monster, knows a bitterness that is incomparable to any sorrow however intense, and only when too late, discovers that it was too dear at any price.

When Jenny Lind was at the height of her career and fame, she suddenly left the stage forever. No explanation was given. The public was left in amaze and wonder. Her income had been enormous, her triumphs the most complete; yet she left it all. Years after, on the shore of the sea, a friend found her late in the afternoon, sitting with a Bible in her lap, looking out into the glory of the sunset. The old question came up of her retirement from the stage in the full blaze of her glory. The singer made this reply: "I retired because every day on the stage made me think less of this, (laying her hand on the Bible in her lap) and nothing at all of that,"

## THE MODERN DEITY.

(pointing to the sunset). What wisdom there is in a conviction like that!

So Wordsworth felt when he lamented,

> "The world is too much with us; late and soon
> Getting and spending, we lay waste our powers."

Whatever is destroying our eternal treasures ought to be given up. Whatever produces a hardening process should be done away with. Whatever obscures the vision to things that are of eternal moment should be removed. Dollars and name will never compensate for the loss of character, and the loss of God. And shall our young women be so enchanted with gold that will, at the very most, but buy life's trinkets, and cry, "I am ready to marry him, to accept his leprous touch if only I may have his money!" And there's the bargain; a bargain of vows comparable only to a Judas kissing the Christ, and as out of place as Satan would be in heaven.

Not only in the higher society, but also in the humbler walks of life we may add, that a money consideration enters into a large proportion of the marriage contract. W. D. Howells depicts the struggles of a woman, who is suddenly left penniless. She sets bravely to work for her self-

## THE MODERN DEITY.

support. She begins by decorating pottery, but her art is so crude that it fails to bring sufficient returns for her needs. Then to the coloring of photographs, then writing for magazines, then millinery, but always with the same disheartening results. She is capable of doing many things, but not capable of doing anything well enough to earn a livelihood, until she tries the humble task of making cheap bonnets for servant girls, and by this she succeeds to eke out a bare existence, till the novelist out of sheer pity, as the only way of extricating her from her trying situation is compelled to marry her off. There are doubtless a great many of such "heroines," young women who can make an impression better than they can make a loaf of bread; vastly more concerned about what goes on the head that in it, and whose only salvation is to be loaded upon some one who can support her. To be compelled to marry, or to cause her parents a sigh of relief when some merciful young man takes the burden off their hands. To marry just for the sake of convenience, is the most humiliating stoop any woman can make—such a marriage is mockery.

But bliss is more frequently quaffed from a granite dipper than from a golden chalise, for love is heaven-born, not made-made. And the

## THE MODERN DEITY.

poor young man with nothing more than health and character and love, who has married the girl whose hands are hardened with toil in the home, the office or the store, has surprised the foolish world, when the things have failed with gold to buy one hour of his heaven-born bliss. When the money consideration is pre-eminent it is the death-dealing blow to happiness. That is one reason why the pitiless storms of evil that have arisen pelting in awful fury against the home, have caused alarm. It is not when death crosses the door-step that tragedy enters, but when truth, and honor, happiness and love are mortgaged for the sake of material gain. Then the costliest wardrobe cannot hide the ghastly skeleton that sits grinning through all the plate and veneer of material show. It is doomed, and the grave-digger stands ready with the spade.

"The night has a thousand eyes, and the day but one,
But the light of the whole world dies with setting sun;
The mind has a thousand eyes and the heart but one,
But the light of the whole life dies when love is done."

## Commercial Patriotism.

We cannot close our eyes to the fact, that in many quarters, devotion to country is measured by money power. Patriotic ideals are obscured by the black clouds of a materialistic philosophy. If one wishes to ascertain how positively empty the proud boast of patriotism is in many a reputed citizen, it is only necessary to present a proposition in which the dollar is concerned. It is said that France uses this as the means by which a man's fitness for army service is tested. In many cases when men are summoned to enlist, they are attacked by diseases of an astonishingly sudden development. Dumbness and deafness being the prevailing afflictions. Appearing before the examining board as a possible recruit, the deaf man positively declares through signs that he can hear nothing, not even the loudest crash of thunder. He is then discharged as unfit, but on leaving the room, an officer follows and drops a gold coin on the pavement behind him; attracted by the magic ring of the coin, he turns to pick it up and is instantly arrested and forced into the service. This is, though unofficial, the test of patriotism in America. Prominent illustrations of it have been before the public eye in recent times. When a beneficent and long-looked-for measure appears in Congress, which in any way threatens to reduce individual dividends, the coin's ring is heard above the call of patriotism. The fact that it will increase the general prosperity matters not; if it is to cut off individual income, then quickly, indeed, the most vigorous protest is made, and love of country goes whistling down the wind and blown into oblivion.

Two of the most far-reaching, vital, patriotic and universally beneficent measures ever proposed, measures long-hoped-for, were those which sought to secure reciprocity with Canada and the United States and for an unlimited arbirtation treaty between Great Britain and the United States. Measures having for their motive the material well-being of the nations concerned, but primarily the putting of all of them upon a basis of brotherhood. While the reciprocity bill passed Congress, it was defeated by the Canadian people. And if we are seeking the reason for its defeat, we shall find it, not that its passage would stagnate the natural resources; nor in the fearfulness of annexation with the United States. No, not in these, primarily. But in this: (and let us give honor to whom honor is due) Canada's good sense vetoed the proposition on the ground that she was unprepared to ally herself to the disturbed, restless and uncertain American business methods. Both of these bills, however, were vigorously opposed by certain American Senators and leading citizens who have been loud in their expressions of patriotism. Why, we ask? This: the measures stepped upon the toes of personal interest. They would decrease the personal profit of a few rich men. They would militate against the pocketbook of some rich pulp growers. Away with the people's welfare; away with the idea of universal peace; what are these considerations compared with the dollar to men who have become mere covetous machines! The men who defeat the will of the people and disregard their rights in legislative halls, are the arch rebels, the traitors of to-day, and shall we permit the compass of our good "ship of state" to be so affected by the proximity of gold as to render it good for nothing? What care we what party badge the political brigand may wear, patriotic devotion demands that he be opposed and deposed, that the people, whether poor or rich, shall be heard, and that the interests of the whole people shall

## THE MODERN DEITY.

be the motive governing our representatives. And we shout in Tennyson's vigorous lines:

> "Oh for a man with heart, head, and hand,
> Like some of the simple great ones gone
>   For ever and ever by;
> One still strong man in a blatant land,
> Whatever they call him, what care I,
> Aristocrat, democrat, autocrat, one
>   Who can rule, and dare not lie."

I have read of an old farmer in the State of Maine who sent a son into the Civil War. He was killed in battle. The old man afterwards expressed his regrets. He said that he had made a great mistake, that he should have had a substitute. He said that he could not get a man anywhere in the country *to do as much work* on the farm as that boy, and that he was the *smallest eater* he ever saw. And in some such degree patriotic ideals are perishing under the dominion of personal gain. What a vivid picture historians have depicted in the marvelous commercial elevation and pinnacle-like position of nations past; (of men as well as nations,) who from the very weight of material accumulation toppled over, unable to maintain that balance essential to perpetuity. What a rebuke in those words of Macaulay, when a delegation presented

## THE MODERN DEITY.

to him a proposition which he could not approve, "Gentlemen," he said, "it is not at all essential that I go to Parliament, but it is absolutely essential that I maintain my *self-respect*." But we are insistent upon reversing that dictum. The ends in immediate view are everything, and self-respect is thrown upon the altar and sacrificed for a base self-interest. It needs another element besides genius, talent or power to rightly guide a people to its highest and most beneficent goal. It calls for men whose large-heartedness stands out conspicuously in all the splendid light of self-efacement against the black background of modern greed. For such a manifestation there is earnest expectation, yes, for this "the whole creation groaneth and travaileth in pain together until now."

> "Were I so tall to reach the pole,
> Or grasp the ocean with my span,
> *I must be measured by my soul;*
> The mind's the measure of the man."

# THE MODERN DEITY.

## The Mad Race for Fun.

Expert economists are constantly telling us that when hard times come upon us, the cause lies deeper than the currency or the tariff. It is found in waste, say they. Who can frame an argument to deny it? Where is there a more extravagant waste than in our follies? "An increase of one-tenth in demand is sufficient to change adversity into prosperity." But what of that when every year we spend, as a nation, more than one-tenth of our product on drink alone? Sixty-three million barrels of beer were sold in the United States during the year ending June 30, 1911, an increase over the preceding year of 6.21%. Our national whisky bill for the same period, was $146,973,000, an increase of nearly $8,000,000, or 5.66%, and this in face of the fact that the spread of prohibition has effected the trade considerably. In a single city of 500,000 inhabitants, no less than $20,000 was spent for champagne alone, and that on a single New Year's Eve. And while the chief city of the land was sending up a dismal wail over the thousands of her poor who go to bed hungry, yet $1,000,000 a

## THE MODERN DEITY.

night is what Gotham spends in revel and pleasure, and in one year New York City could spare $45,000,000 to spend at Coney Island, her great temple of fun, an amount six times what the United States paid for Alaska, and three times what was paid Napoleon for Louisiana. Who can measure what this would mean to our industries in the production of life's necessities? Factories would be literally swamped with orders, the hungry would be fed, and the bare feet shod. What we pay for our follies is greatly in excess of what we lack in life's necessities. It

> "* * * * drains our cellars dry,
> And keeps our larder clean; puts out our fires,
> And introduces hunger, frost, and woe,
> Where peace and hospitality might reign."

The New York Times published the following story, told by General Chaffee at a reception given in his honor by the militiamen at Poughkeepsie: Not long ago a soldier in the regular army stopped me on the street and asked me to lend him a quarter.

"Why, yesterday you received your month's pay, did you not?" I asked.

"Yes," replied the veteran.

"Where's your money now?"

## THE MODERN DEITY.

"It's like this," he went on. "I met a friend and we had dinner. I was mightily surprised when the bill was $8. Then I bought $1 worth of cigars, and we went to the theater for $4. After the theater we went down the Bowery, and I spent $2 there."

"That's $15," I replied. "What happened to that other 50 cents?"

The old fellow seemed puzzled. Finally he answered:

"I must have spent that *foolishly.*"

In the mad race for fun how dearly men pay for the worthless prize! The creed of the deluded worshipper at this shrine, "Let us eat, drink and be merry," is the spade that digs the grave for all that is best in manhood and womanhood. The only question in their catechism: "What is the chief end of man?" "To have a good time and seek fun forever," is that which leads its blind devotees to spend exhorbitant amounts in rearing and maintaining its colossal temples with a liberality that puts Christendom to shame. That if a woman can lose enough sleep at parties to be sick all the day long, she is having the best time in her life; and that if a man can put in his time at midnight orgies that will unfit him for the day's duty, he is at the top-notch of human happiness. A standing head-line in Paris newspapers is, "Drames Passionels"—Tragedies from Passion. When the Germans invaded the city and the thunder of cannon roared through the streets, the people were engaged in witnessing plays in the theaters. And knowing what was going on without, yet wholly unconcerned, they rose en masse and shrieked, "Shut the doors and let the play go on." Alas! Fox's "Book of Martyrs" would look like a penny pamphlet compared with the book that might be written of "Folly's Book of Martyrs," composed of the no less thrilling stories of the multitudes slain upon the altar of the goddess of fun.

# THE MODERN DEITY.

## Vanitas Omnia Vanitas.

Cleveland Moffett makes a fearful indictment on "The Shameful Misuse of Wealth." When the wife of a millionaire gives a banquet costing $50,000, the floral decorations alone costing $5,000. When there are women who spend on clothes for poodle dogs $1,000 per annum; coats lined with ermine at $200 a piece, in which is a dear little pocket for the precious little poodle's handkerchief; for boots of many colored leathers $5 to $10 a pair, and topped out with a collar, like a bejeweled necklace, set with precious stones and valued at many hundreds of dollars. When sickness befalls the dear thing, a specialist is hurried to his bedside, and we are told that there are fashionable dog doctors who sleep with a telephone close to the ear, lest his canine majesty die before medical skill arrives; while the only perceptible difference between the faithful watchdog which has nothing but fidelity to commend him, and the poodle dressed like a Queen Anne, is the vanity of its owner, who would say with pitiable, yet characteristic weakness, "I paid $3,000 for the heavenly creature." When death overtakes

## THE MODERN DEITY.

him, he is put in a satin-lined coffin, followed to the grave by his heart-broken mistress and burried with human honors. In the face of such revelations we must wonder if we have gotten as far away from the extravangant vanities which characterized the times of the Caesars as we are wont to suppose; and when we go still further and find that with vanity as the toastmaster of their extravagant feasts, we should temper our criticism of heathen Rome or of the days of Louis XIV, with the flavor of our own imitation of them. But the thing is far from amusing when we know that six hundred men go astray in a year as embezzlers, robbing the people of $25,000,000 in the vain effort to keep up expensive homes. And all this on the same principle, as some one has expressed it, "The only thing that keeps a lot of us from having a motor car, is the fact that we haven't anything to mortgage." Surely there is some truth in the statement that "luxury is the spade that has dug the grave of every nation that ever perished."

Frivolity has been named as the besetting sin of womanhood. The general rule is in no way affected by the fact that there are many noble and notable exceptions. "To amuse and be amused, to see and be seen, to follow in the train of fashion and turn life into a pageant or a song." What a mockery of the responsibilities of life!

> "She that will eat her breakfast in her bed,
> And spend the morn in dressing of her head,
> And sit at dinner like a maiden bride,
> And talk of nothing but of pride;
> God in His mercy may do much to save her,
> But what a case is he in that shall have her."

The only end of such existence is a tombstone bearing the pathetic inscription: "Vanity of Vanities."

A husband who was reprimanded by his wife for looking about the church during prayer, said, "I was just counting to see if there were as many women closing their eyes as there were eyeing their clothes." Caring more for dress than disposition, troubled more by an unfashionable hat than a neglected God, talking more with their dressmaker than with the Creator, and following the fashion-plate more closely than the Saviour. It reminds us of Biddy at her wedding. Patrick had on lavender trousers, and his first kid gloves, lavender too, and a new silk hat he know not what to do with. And Biddy was arrayed in splendor, with a vast picture-hat of the most picturesque, surmounted by a peck of roses that vied with the damask of her cheek. As they went

## THE MODERN DEITY.

up the aisle, Biddy trod on golden clouds. As they knelt at the altar, as they sat before it while mass was said, as they walked down the aisle, she caught glances, through her modestly downcast lashes, of admiration that gave her sighs of rapture. At the door stood the populace, in assorted sizes and ages, applauding, and there was an open barouche adorned with streamers of white ribbon. As they rode away, Biddy leaned her head on Patrick's shoulder, regardless of the picture-hat, and said out of the fulness of her bursting heart: "O Paddy dear, wouldn't it be hivenly if we could just sthand on the sidewalk and see oursilves go by!" "A dream," some might call her, while in truth we would say "She's a hideous nightmare." Peacock-like and just as silly, for

"The stupid sheep and silkworms wore
That very clothing long before."

Or what Emerson has called, "Sugar plums and cat's cradles, the toilet, compliments, quarrels, cards and custards, which rack the wit of all society;" people whose whole life is really concerned with, what he says, the one question, "What joys has kind nature provided for us dear creatures?" Frivolity at its highest development, and how silly it all is, to see what F. W. Robertson calls "the spirit of childhood carried into manhood," grown men and grown women, and the women no more than the men, for as one has observed, "I'm not denyin' the women are foolish, but God Almighty made 'em to match the men," still playing with their toys, their dolls and hoops, only the toys are called by a different name, such as dress and dine, fun and fame, and what Browning in "The Lost Leader" has pictured as the blinding dust to nobler things:

> "Just for a handful of silver, he left us,
> Just for a ribbon to stick in his coat."

And we heartily agree with what Ruskin says in one of his essays: "A butterfly is much more free than a bee; but you honor the bee more, because it is subject to certain laws, which fit it for orderly function in bee society." For what can be comparable to that slavery in which the butterfly of society is chained? We rehearse stories of Siberian atrocity until our blood runs cold. But there is one, but one absolute monarch —the czar of human opinion. The edict which he issues drags the will-o-the-whisp into a Siberian of littleness only faintly typified by the degradation of exile among those Asiatic moun-

## THE MODERN DEITY.

tains. The fashion of the world exiles finest thought; dungeons truest manhood and womanhood; rivets chain and ball on our loftiest aspirations; makes our feet fast in the stocks of its whims. It so vetoes independence that we dare not be free and genuine. Alas! there are none more abject slaves than they who are in slavery to things. Verily did the Master say, "The life is more than meat, and the body than raiment, for after all these things do the heathen seek."

# THE MODERN DEITY.

## God Still on the Field.

The reason that some have branded the age as godless, is not that He is out of relation with it; that He has set it agoing, as one might start a machine, but left it to run itself according to established laws, or after its own wild will. Or as Tennyson pictures in the "Lotus Eaters," with the gods enjoying their nectar, and smiling at the sorrows and the woes of men. No, He has not left it, nor has He removed Himself from the fellowship of men.

> "He is no fable old nor mystic lore,
>   Nor dream of bards and seers,
> No dead fact stranded on the shore
>   Of the oblivious years.
>
> But warm, sweet, tender even yet,
>   A present help is He;
> And faith has still its Olivet
>   And love its Galilee."

Ah, yes, He is still present. But men do not give Him a chance to reveal His interest in and love for them. Life is lived at such high pressure in these days; from morn till night, driven from pillar to post, and thus the days run on, and the weeks glide by, and the years slip away, when, lo, we are out of the world before we rightly know that we are in it. And yet, miracle of miracles, God is always wanting to talk to man. In the midst of this all-too busy life, crushed by the malling fury of business, God stands waiting, waiting for an audience with man. And while a thousand interests crowd and clamor for a hearing, God waits, standing, as it were, and leaning His hand on man's shoulder and saying, "A word with you." The Creator wanting to talk with the creature; God waiting, patiently waiting, for a word with man; the heavenly Father asking an audience with His earthly child! What infinite condescension! What sublime stooping! And because we are so pre-occupied, what a time He has to have a word with us, and it is only when He talks out loud that He gets our ear, then we think we hear Him. Elijah-like we hear the hurricane, roaring and crashing and tearing by; and the earthquake that shakes the earth and quivers among the hills; and the fire, scorching and burning and devastating; but God was not in these, awe-inspiring and thought-provoking though they seemed. But it is in the "still small voice" that He is heard. He does speak out loud if He cannot otherwise divert our attention, and we, I trust, may still hear the echo of it in those outspoken events in our history. But we may be sure that it is only when men will not hear that He enjoins us with some Sinai or Jerusalem fall, and this is because we are so deaf. Nobody can help hearing the clamorous and the gustatory, but it is the gentler method that He wishes to prevail, the method of the "quiet talk."

> "Unheard, because our ears are dull,
> Unseen, because our eyes are dim,
> He walks the earth—the Wonderful—
> And all great deeds are done for Him."

In 1861 when a minister wrote Secretary Chase of the United States Treasury in reference to some recognition of God in our national currency, Mr. Chase immediately wrote the director of the Mint in these words: "No nation can be strong except in the strength of God, and this truth should be declared in our currency." And out of this came the inscription on our coins, "In God We Trust." In recent years, for good and sufficient reasons, as he thought, Mr. Roosevelt directed that this inscription should be done away. At this the whole land was wrought up to a state of ferment which flooded Congress with such monster petitions and memorials, that the words were at once restored. This may well be taken as an expression by the people, in the belief that it not the gold mined in California or Klondike, not the crisp greenbacks with the governmental guarantee written across their face, not our army nor our fleets of grim gray battleships that constitute the bulwarks of our land, nor protect us from imminent disaster, but to lose God in the midst of these things, to lose that sensitiveness of conscience which enables us to properly label right and wrong, to lose these, there is nothing that will save us.

> "Far called our navies melt away;
> On dune and headland sinks the fire;
> Lo! all the pomp of yesterday
> Is one with Ninevah and Tyre.
> Judge of the nations, spare us yet,
> Lest we forget! Lest we forget!"

## The Christian Church.

The much-discussed and now time-worn phrase, "What's the matter with the Church?" is, after all, a fallacious and an all-misleading question, as though the trend of the times must be laid at her door. It is a very common sin of humanity to blame others rather than to blame oneself. The people who continually find fault with other's faults, seldom find fault with their own fault. Adam blamed Eve, Eve blamed the serpent, the serpent blamed the devil, the elder son blamed the younger, and none of them blamed themselves. In a similar way, the Church is constantly having thrust at her such interrogations as these: "Why is the Church not more attractive?" "Other institutions draw, why does the Church fail?" "What has happened to her once honored power?" "Why has she lost her grip of the masses?" And to this end remedial advise has poured into the Church in a copious and perennial stream, dividing itself into two prominent channels, viz.:

Secularize the Church. Only make the church

as much like a grand palace of worldly amusement as possible; let her pulpit ministrations be in the hands of a Lyceum Bureau, her music in the control of an opera manager, and then she will see the people flocking to her altar like doves to their windows.

Spiritualize the Church! We are constantly being told, by those who at least, profess to know, "preach the pure and simple Gospel and the churches will be filled." But men who know, have grown weary of such blatant ignorance, because it isn't true, and there never was a time when it was less true than now. The Gospel is the thing people do not want. Indeed, there is vastly more of this type of preaching in our evangelical pulpits than is usually credited to them, and churches where "gospel preaching" is the weekly attraction are by no means "pushed" for room.

The truth is, however, that any church can be filled by any or all of the following features, and when they have been put in operation have secured the desired end: a prima donna in the choir; a vaudeville on the platform; an acrobatic clown in the pulpit, or cake and coffee in the refectory. These will scarcely ever fail to draw. They will ever appeal to the throng that finds its religion in the comic pages of the Sunday paper, and that decides its heaven or its hell in accordance with the scores of the baseball returns. But the people of higher aspirations and worthier ideals, these are the people in every community who seek the Church, and there find answer to the conscious hunger of their immortal souls. The godless do not go to church. It has no interest to them. A show to them is better. And while we are in no way pronouncing a wholesale condemnation upon these things as essentially evil, in themselves, nor advocating as reactionists, a restoration of Puritanic days, to stagnate in some sleepy-hollow and dream our lives away in some realm of ethereal bliss! No, not that. But the Church is not going into competition with the world in affording attractions which appeal to the carnality of the crowd who have, forsooth, put out their spiritual eyes, and closed their understanding ears to the vision and the voice of higher things. Indeed, there is nothing in psychology truer than what George Eliot has said, "You cannot entertain God and the devil on the same floor and on equal terms." And while the Church is prophesied to lose in the spectacular display of the crowd, the Church which cares more to woo a soul than to court a grin can well afford to lose, when such a loss is her truest gain.

Perhaps the cause of her so-called weakness, if that is the accusation, may be said to lie in the fact, that whenever she has attempted to do her Lord's work with the devil's tools, she has invariably been shorn of her power. That the modern deity has in many instances crept into her fold, is pitiable but true. Many churches are little more than social organizations of baptized worldlings, who care nothing for either creed or deed. The building to be "modern" must have a well-appointed kitchen, dining-room and parlor wherein to eat, drink and be merry, and to entertain those who "mind earthly things." Those who absent themselves from the prayer meetings and other spiritual services of the church, are sure to be on hand when a "good time" is announced, then it is that the church draws—the "wood, hay and the stubble" are in conspicious evidence—the combustible material; while the meetings purely for worship are attended by "the faithful few"—and these are the "gold, silver and precious stones"—the enduring fabric out of which the Kingdom of God is built. And is it not all too true, that there are even ministers who give messages to classes—sometimes to this class and then to that—and instead of "rightly dividing the word of truth" cut it on the bias to suit what people want, rather than what they need? Like the divinity student of whom I read. He went from the seminary to preach a trial sermon, and, on his return, was greeted by one of the professors with, "How did you get on with your sermon?" "First rate, first rate," said the young man. "What was your text?" asked the professor. "How shall we escape if we neglect so great salvation." "A good text," said the professor. "How did you treat it?" "First," said the student, "I showed 'em how great this salvation is." "That's excellent," said the man of wisdom, beaming his approval with face wreathed in smiles. "And, second, I showed 'em how to escape if they neglected it." And there are those who, by their catering methods, are doing little else than that, and exercising their gifts in such a way as to further the success of an entrenched godlessness.

There is no "Conflict between religion and the church" as some magazine writers would have us believe. A dislike for religious things is the disease with which the age is terribly afflicted, manifesting itself in a cold indifference to the Church, the Church which has ever stood

## THE MODERN DEITY.

as the champion of our priceless liberties and the protector of all our human rights. With all the railing accusations, both of friends and foes, the Church is still the power to which we look in the manufacture of character, and without which, the community would be a sorry place indeed. The sea captain who, when he came to the village on the sea coast, insisted on paying $10 to the church, although he did not attend himself, was asked his reasons for so doing, and said, that he had been in the habit of carrying cargoes of oysters and clams from that place, and found, since the church was built, the people were more honest than they used to be, for before the church was built, he often found the cargo, when he came to count it, a thousand clams short. That there is a power in a living Christianity, which even its enemies are unable to deny, can be seen in such characters as Charteris, a notorious scoundrel of his time, who once said to a man distinguished for his religious principles, "I would give a thousand pounds to have your good character." And when asked why, replied, "Because I could make ten thousand pounds by it." Indeed, scoffers have sometimes been the first to fall upon their knees when danger overwhelmed them, and after it had passed, laugh at themselves for such pro-

## THE MODERN DEITY.

testations of piety. As old Seneca said, "They deny God by day, but own Him at night," and all the arguments which men have used against the Church and her teachings have melted away in the season of their extremity.

But character is not a matter of circumstantial evidence. It does not consist in having a Bible in the house in case of sickness, quoting scripture in defense of personal aggrandizement, (the devil does that) nor even in paying the preacher, any more than having a sword, or reciting the Constitution or paying taxes makes a man a soldier

> A man may cry 'Christ! Christ!'
> With no more piety than other people;
> A crow's not counted a religious bird
> Because it keeps a-cawing from a steeple."

Sincerity must ever be its test. Nor is it found in what Gratiano said,

"I will put on a sober habit,
Talk with respect, wear prayer-book in my pocket look demurely,
Nay more, while grace is saying, hood mine eyes thus with my hat and sigh and say, 'Amen.'"

To pose under the guise of the genuine, is to build a reputation on the cheap unrealities of life. While this is so, what shall we say of the

## THE MODERN DEITY.

frightful picture one might draw, on the impending calamities of the unchurched multitudes, who think no more of God? Think of the mighty army to whom the church has no attraction! Imagine a world without God! Conscience as dead as a lifeless form, and the soul virtually buried beneath the derbis of evil inclinations. Tennyson has drawn that picture in his "Holy Grail," and VanDyke in his "Blue Flower," but for a real picture you must read Carlyle's "Bloody Days of the French Revolution," and there you see the inevitable result of a people logically trying to live without God. Goths in feelings, and Vandals in customs, must be the only end of the mass of the unchurched, who while the ringing of the church bells calls the devout to prayer and praise, but signals them to their god-forgotten mirth and orgies. No God, no soul, no Sabbath, retribution but the figment of the inflamed imagination, and heaven though grand, only a vast delusion.

History is still repeating itself in this fact, that the Church has, ever and anon, felt the fluctuations of the impoverishment and prosperity of the periods through which she has passed, the ebb and flow of material weal and woe have been constantly throbbing through her life. It has been demonstrated all along the years, that the world's stringent times have been her best times; that the seasons of the closed shop and the poor crop was and is the seasons when her spiritual thermometer registers highest. It is when we are in the midst of plenty that God sees little of us, and because we have no desire to see much of Him. When the flour barrel is all but empty, and the hungry wolf stands grinning at the door, we are then quite willing to discount our independency of God and creep up close to His all-forgotten love. Such people are constantly reversing what one said to a friend, "When you see me getting prosperous, pray for my soul." Therein lies the danger. While poverty may not be the greatest calamity, prosperity may be the greatest curse. The material prosperity of men has never been conducive to the highest interests of the Church, nor can we say vital to her real life. And because religion has been so largely buried beneath the debris of "things" in the prosperous life of the many, the accusation that the Church has lost her power is groundless. Let blight, depression, disaster, or money-panic occur, and the noisy alarmist has suddenly turned dumb.

And yet, men surrounded by all the charms of

## THE MODERN DEITY.

luxury, having every wish gratified, and every desire fulfilled, they walk the earth the moving monuments of woe. The facts are all against the supposition that happiness depends upon material wealth. It has been frequently shown, that the more prosperous a man is, the fewer were his hours of pleasure. The man who has thousands at his command, who is enabled to view extensive fields, watch for an upward flight in stocks, cannot have the happiness of the common day laborer, who owns not the roof which covers him, and who scarcely knows how long he shall have food for his children. The one may have much coin, but it is mingled with crushing care. The other, may have penury, but it is mingled with peace. The one trusts in the income of his stocks, in the safety of his investments; the other, is more likely to trust in God who heareth the young ravens when they cry, and looks for food and raiment to the

"Glorious Giver, who doeth all things well."
The highest pinnacle of earthly ambition has been attained, but the "aching void" has not been filled. The loudest blast of fame's burnished trumpet, cannot make melody to a heart oppressed with sorrow and bowed with grief. All the gold found in newly discovered mines, cannot

# THE MODERN DEITY.

drive away sorrow's unbidden tear that rushes into the temple of the soul. These are but the outer scaffolding; within is the real structure. To bodily interests there must be added an undefined plus, and to this higher self man owes his chief duty and his utmost solicitation, because all other responsibilities, whatever they are, focus there. These outer things are often like the feathers of the jay, and the skin of the adder. The pleasant plumage does not make the one sing more sweetly; the painted skin does not detract from the poisonous nature of the other. An inner nature hungers for food which cannot be appeased with the fruits of the labor of one's hands or the genius of one's mind; its nourishment is not crushed from earthly seeds, nor its covering woven in earthly looms.

# THE MODERN DEITY.

## Heart Hunger.

All of the foregoing has been said to simply show that the poor, befooled and silly world in its sober moments, knows full well that its buying and selling, its eating and drinking, its getting and having, this game of life, does not compass life's scheme, unless we must prove to men that they have souls. Tell a man today that he has a soul and he will think you are crazy, and regard your proffered information as an insult to his intelligence. Man has a tripartite nature. In common with the animal he has, on the lowest plane, a material body. That which differentiates him from all other forms of organisms, however, is the fact that he is possessed of a spirit in the similitude of God. While on the mediate plane he is endowed with a living and rational soul, the nexus between body and spirit. Each department, or nature, must be fed with nutriment adapted to its need—the material body with the chemical, the mind with thought and the spirit with God. When the physical degenerates into a prodigal, leaves the Father's table to roam in the far-country and feds among the swine of sensual and voluptuous indulgence, then the scared temple of the body is overrun with thieves. When the soul pushes back its chair from the banqueting-table of honor, truth and virtue, and goes forth to breathe the miasma in the swamps of envy, greed, self-seeking, and all that is scorned by our better instincts, then the curtains have been drawn on the windows against the light, and the darkness of the darkest night has come. And when the spirit which constantly clamors for its native diet, its craving answered only by denial of converse with God and communion with heaven, life's greatest tragedy has occurred and the obituary of the spirit is written, for death, more tragic than that which knocks with icy knuckles at our home door, must be the inevitable result.

It is this immortal hunger, oftentimes coming confusingly, indeed, upon men, which makes all mere things too childish to satisfy. An inexplicable longing comes a-tugging at the heart, which seems to say that life has loftier, yea, moral values; that the world of bread for the body is but the one-half of life, and its meanest half at that. It comes to all men, sometime, when worldly interests make us positively weary, and feel like the old and dissipated Marquis of

## THE MODERN DEITY.

Queensbury who would sit in his fine house at Twickenham and, looking out on the Thames, murmuring so pleasantly along, could only say, "I am sick of hearing people praise that eternal river; it does nothing but flow, flow, flow." Or, like the gay Lord Chesterfield, who said, "I have run the silly rounds of business and pleasure, and have done with them all. I have enjoyed all the pleasures of the world, and consequently know their futility, and do not regret their loss. I appraise them at their real value, which is very low; whereas those who have not experienced them always overrate them. They only see the gay outside and are dazzled with the glare; but I have been behind the scenes and have seen all the coarse pulleys and dirty ropes which exhibit and move the gaudy machine. I have seen and smelt the tallow candles which illuminate the whole decorations, to the astonishment and admiration of an ignorant audience. I look back on all that is past as one of those romantic dreams which opium commonly produces, and I have no wish to repeat the nauseous dose. Shall I say that I bear this with resignation? No, I bear it because I must, whether I will or no. I think of nothing but killing time the best way I can, now that it has become my enemy." What a melancholy confession, from a man who had everything, one would think, that earth could provide to make one happy!

It has been proved over and over again and from times immemorial, that things external cannot secure permanent peace and pleasure.

*"The conscious mind is its own awful world,"*

and if this be in commotion no outward circumstance, however beautiful and pleasing, can give it rest. The Koran of Mohammed has this strange fable about Abraham. When he set out upon his journeys, he had no knowledge of religious truth. He looked up and saw the evening star and said to his followers, "That is my God." But the star went down, and he said, "I care not for any gods that set." By and by the grand constellations appeared, and he said, "These are my gods." But the galaxies of stars were carried beneath the west; and again he said, "I will have no gods that set." But the moon arose, and he exclaimed, "This is my god." But the moon, too, went down. Then, when the sun arose he saluted it as Divine; but the wheeling sky carried the king of day away behind the pine-tops of the rosy-tinted west. Then Abraham, in the holy twilight, turning his face upward

## THE MODERN DEITY.

toward the serene and tranquil empyrean, exclaimed, "I give myself to Him who was, and is, and is to come, Father of the sun and moon and stars, who never sets, for He only is the everlasting Light."

What then is the antidote to the disease of the age? It was a wise word, indeed, that Apollodorus placed over the entrance of his studio:

> "'Tis no hard thing to reprehend me,
> But let the man that blames me mend me."

How are we to resist the prevailing influences of the times? How escape the hardening process of the age? In the most logical way, to be sure. We resist the contagion of an epidemic, the stealthy grip of a malaria, by the reserve power of an abundant vitality, by fortifying the powers of life, by buttressing the life within. We are to remember that "the life is more than meat." That a man's life does not consist "in the abundance of his possessions." And as George Macdonald has so well put it, "To have what we want is riches, but to be able to do without is power." Many of the world's great saints are among its poor, with few of its luxuries. A coarse and patched garment may cover their bodies, but a costly white robe enwraps their souls. They may

## THE MODERN DEITY.

sojourn in a humble cabin, but they dwell in a mansion. They may lunch on a crust, but they feast at a banquet. They may be embiciles in body, but strong in soul; feeble in intellect, but healthful in heart; despised of men, but honored of God. In their external appearance there may be absolutely nothing for the world to envy; but in their character and prospects there is something for angels to admire. At their funeral there may be few to mourn, the casket of a plain and simple covering, but the contents are precious jewels to God. The man who gets and holds the mountains of earth's possessions may think he has the game of life all his way; but the man of power, the man who "can do without," will have his innings.

And thank God, there are such still. The world stands back and wonders how they can so easily set aside that for which the multitudes make their chief object—the "bread" which the world values so highly. The Divine Master expressed it in answer to the wondering disciples, when He said, "I have meat to eat that ye know not of"—in possession of an inner satisfaction which the world knows nothing about. Such an one partakes of a hidden manna, the meat of whose strength lesser and ignoble souls are absolutely ignorant. To repose in inglorious ease, to conform for comfort's sake, to tone down conscience and seek the husks upon which prodigals from God's will must feed, is only to discover in the awakening, that they have sold themselves for naught, and labored for that which satisfieth not. But the banquet which the Christ provides for the soul's eternal nourishment is that alone which will secure for men immunity to the seductive temptations, the attractive and fascinating idols of the world. For the Kingdom of God and His righteousness are infintely worthy of our seeking, it puts things in their proper place, it instructs us how to use the world without abusing it, and business, commerce, fun, fame and money, even success itself, shall minister to us, but not enslave us; shall embellish life, but not absorb it, and perchance, add all these *things* to our possessions, and yet leave strong and pure within the life of God.

Robert Burns never wrote a truer word than that which he sent to a friend:

> "When rantin' roun' in pleasure's ring,
>   Religion may be blinded;
> But if she gie a random sting,
>   But little may be minded.
> But when on life we're tempest-tossed,
>   And conscience but a canker,
>   *A correspondence fixed wi' Heaven*
>   Is sure a noble anchor."

## THE MODERN DEITY.

This "correspondence fixed wi' heaven," this is the bulwark against which the fiercest tides of life may beat but not destroy; the strength that will withstand the onslaughts of every tempting bit of "bread" the world may throw before our eyes; the "anchor of the soul" that will hold both sure and steadfast. So said Mr. Gladstone: "Whatever I may think of the pursuits of industry and science, and of the triumphs and glories of art, I do not mention any one of these as the great specific for alleviating the sorrows of human life, and encountering the evils which deface the world. If I am asked what is the remedy for the deepest sorrows of the human heart, what a man should chiefly look to in his progress through life, as the power that is to sustain him under trials, and enable him manfully to confront his afflictions, I must point to something very different—to something which, in a well-known hymn, is called 'The Old, Old Story,' told of in an old, old Book, and taught with an old, old teaching, which is the greatest gift ever given to mankind." To what must men turn, disheartened, remorseful and all but disgusted, in the hour when disaster descends with its overwhelming and merciless cruelties, only to what too many turn as their only alternative,

## THE MODERN DEITY.

"Anywhere, anywhere, out of the world.'"

Or, as the ragged urchin put it, whom a good man met in the street, and, putting his hand on his head, said: "My little man, when your father and your mother forsake you, who will take you up?" And with characteristic innocence the lad replied, "The perlice, sir." And this may well be taken as the prevailing logic of the times. A rank atheism knows of nothing better in the hour of distress. And may God pity the age which can turn to nothing else in its time of deepest trials than that which incites to a diatribe against the Almighty, or takes upon itself the responsibility of its own self-destruction!

THE MODERN DEITY.

### Back to the Father.

This can be the only prescription. If the age which moves slow finds God, the balm for its ugly wounds; and gets glimpses of another world, even a heavenly, the lotion for its wearied eyes; and hears, even faintly, the voice that spoke into being the things that are; if sorrowing and suffering men and women feel the omnipotent yet gentle arm of a Father folding them in His bosom, and hushing the tempests of their sad and aching hearts into eternal calm with the lullaby of His heavenly peace, is the age not more fortunate; more eminently and pre-eminently prosperous than the age which boasts of having astonished the wildest dreams of the mystic, merely by the swiftness of its movement, or the multiplication of its wealth? Such holy ambition is the only one worthy of our manhood and womanhood. To leave God out of the reckoning, the God in whose image and likeness we were created, is to be unworthy of our birthright. Let us remember that we are still the children of a Heavenly Father. When one of the sovereigns of France was approached with a re-

## THE MODERN DEITY.

quest to sign a dishonorable measure, he answered, "The blood of Charlemagne runs through my veins. How dare you thus affront me?" And we read that Themistocles was asked one day by one of his soldiers why he did not gather the spoils which the enemy had left behind in their sudden flight, and in answer said, "Thou mayest, for thou art not Themistocles." And when a man thoughtfully considers his Divine lineage and listens to the call of God's voice, he will ever regard as beneath him that for which the thoughtless throng scramble to secure. And like the pilgrim in Bunyan's immortal allegory, escaping from the City of Destruction with the vision of heaven looming up before him ran with all his might, and stuffing his fingers into his ears that he might shut out the dissuading voices of friends and kinsmen, cried, *"Life! Life! Eternal Life!"*

Alfred Lord Tennyson was born in a parsonage. In college he fell on evil days when doubts shut out his horizon. But death taking away Arthur Hallam, his gifted friend, struck the sun out of his sky. It was standing by the fast failing breath, however, that he listened to that confession of heart-hunger and the secret of its satisfaction when the dying man said: "Lord, I

## THE MODERN DEITY.

have viewed this world all over. I have tried how this thing or that will fit my spirit. I can find nothing to rest on; for nothing here hath any rest itself. Oh, Blessed Jesus—center of light and strength—I come back and join myself to Thee and to Thee alone." And out of his pain and anguish, his doubts vanished, and Tennyson climbed "up the world's altar stairs that slope through darkness up to God." It is said of Louis XIV. that he was the richest and most powerful monarch in Europe. His country palace of St. Germain was the most luxurious in external architecture and of internal adornment which it was possible for wealth to procure. Fountains played throughout his groves and blooming gardens and verdent lawns, while through the valley below, like a strip of silver ribbon wound the River Seine. Only a few miles to the north lay Paris, the beautiful. But like the Prince of Abyssinia, in happy valley, Louis was never happy. Indeed, he dreaded to go there, and while there he was constantly watched and hurried away as soon as possible. Why? Ah, only a few miles to the northwest the great cathedral of St. Dennis always stared into his face. There was the massive tower which he could not avoid seeing. Beneath that tower were the

## THE MODERN DEITY.

gloomy vaults of the kings of France. He could not endure the sight, yet could not escape it. Whether he stepped upon the balcony or peered out of the window, by sunlight or by moonlight, there rose the lofty spire of St. Dennis, pointing to the final tribunal and silently saying, "You, too, must die." Well, he abandoned Saint Germain and reared for himself a splendid mansion at Versailles, where the haunting specter of St. Dennis' tower was no longer in view. Yet he was none the happier. Poor Louis, it was not the gloomy tower with its vaults of the dead beneath that caused his unrest! No, not that. But a far deeper reality which he had failed to discover.

> "This world can never give
> The rest for which we sigh;
> 'Tis not the whole of life to live,
> Nor all of death to die."

It is the soul's story in every age. The body may find its satisfaction in things. The raven which Noah sent forth found satisfaction in the carcasses of the dead floating upon the great waste, and so never returned. Not so the dove. It came back, finding no rest but in the confines of the ark. The soul is dovelike in this, that it cannot find in things the satisfaction

## THE MODERN DEITY.

which its pure and holy intention demands, and finds it not until it rests in the ark of God. Stories of famine in India, or the starving multitudes in Russia would grow pale before the heart-breaking tale of the soul, should it tell its pathetic story. Here is the modern parable of life. The man is holding a dialogue with his soul. "Soul, I have much goods laid up for many years; I have a magnificent farm and a clear title to it. I have it well stocked with flocks the rarest. The barns are all new. By my industry and diligence my crops have yielded an hundred fold, and since I pulled down the old barns and built greater, the granaries contain enough for time to come. I take pride in saying that I am greatly pleased at what I have done. Now, soul, I want to lay all at thy feet; come and join me in a life of ease from care, a life of wholesale indulgence; come, "Soul, take thine ease; let us eat, drink and be merry."

Now the soul has something to say: "Man, thou surely meanest well, as man, but your words are insulting; you are either ignorant, debased or a fool. You evidently underestimate me, for I am infinitely above 'enlarged barns' and bursting granaries. I, a soul, would starve to death if doomed to subsist on these. You seek to degrade me, to brutalize me. 'Much goods' is all you have to offer me, and what will 'goods' do for me, even 'much goods,' before the great and final tribunal? I can get along famously without your 'goods,' but I shall fail utterly, an eternal bankrupt without God. And as for 'ease' with which you would entice me, there is no such thing as ease to a living and an abounding soul. My native sphere is not in ease, but to climb—

"Climbing up new Calvarys ever
With the Cross that turns not back."

Your selfish comfort and pleasure are the great ends for which, you think, the universe exists. Your personal pronouns of "my barns," "my goods," have altogether shut God out of your reckoning. And while you are gleefully calculating on taking your ease, eating, drinking and making merry, listen, *"thou fool!* this night thy soul shall be required of thee, then whose shall these be which thou hast laid up?" When God calls a man a "fool" he never rallies from the indictment. And the man who thinks he carries the key to heaven in bank vault or pants pocket will find that it fits the wrong door. Such a man cannot enjoy the money he has on earth; he can't take it with him; and if he could it would

## THE MODERN DEITY.

do him no good—it would burn. And like Alexander the Great, who, when he came to die, directed that he should be buried with his hands outside his shroud, so that all might see that of all he had come to possess he carried none of it away with him.

In the old cathedral at Elgin, there is a quaint epitaph, carved on a slab on the wall:

"This world is a city full of streets;
And death is the market that all men meets;
If life were a thing that money could buy,
The poor could not live and the rich would not die."

If a man without a body would be a ghost, a man without a mind would be a fool, it is perfectly within the lines of logic to say that a man without a religious life would be a brute. You need more than paint and brush and palette to make a picture—you need light. You need more than pen, ink and paper to write a book—you need brains. You need more than food, raiment and gymnastics to build a body—you need air. You need more to make a man than physical elements or the knowledge of the senses—you cannot make manhood without a soul, and the soul is the sixth sense to which Infinite power is

## THE MODERN DEITY.

vouchsafed, and which alone can give life value. Human life needs a helmsman. It needs a moral dynamic. It needs an extra-human energy to counteract the current. It needs a force within to breast the drift. In a word, it needs God in the life, and He is all that and more. And it is "every word that proceedeth out of the mouth of God" that must give to life its meaning, if it is to have any meaning at all. This is what Tennyson meant when he said:

> "For what are men better than sheep or goats,
> If, knowing God, they lift not hands of prayer?"

Let us be sure that all the unrest of nations, the clamor against existing evils, the ceaseless throbbing of its confusing strife, the mad rush to and fro among mankind, is but the outward expression of an inward craving, a desire for better and higher things than they now possess, an unsatisfied hunger which nothing else can ever put to rest. A hungering and a thirsting after something, shall we say, a righteousness? Yes, for beneath all other hungers, down, far down in the secret recesses of the soul whose hallowed courts no one may tread but ourselves and God, down there buried ever so deeply that it oftentimes eludes our knowledge, there lies a hunger,

## THE MODERN DEITY.

not consciously righteous, perhaps, yet none the less real, a craving after that which will alone bring to the life its heritage of tranquility and its legacy of peace. A peace that is as calm as a river. The peace of Him who said: "Peace I leave with you; My peace I give unto you, not as the world giveth, give I unto you." The heathen, ignorant of the true and the living God, seeks to satisfy this same human longing, this same divine instinct in dreary and long-continued prostrations before his man-made idol, for

> "In even savage bosoms
> There are longings, yearnings, strivings
> For the good they comprehend not."

And all these strange, undefined and restless movements of men, these eager and unhallowed aspirations, if rightly interpreted, would but reveal them to be a panting of the soul after God. For

> "One accent of the Holy Ghost
> The heedless world hath never lost."

And to get back to Him who said, "I am the Bread of Life," this is the secret of inexhaustible happiness, the unquestionable answer to our human cravings, and the ultimate satisfaction of every life. It is written, "Man shall not live by bread alone, but by every word that proceedeth out of the mouth of God." It was true in the history of Israel; true in the beginning of the Christian era; true now. It was a devil that attempted to discount it; it is demoniacal to do so now. And in a time when the life of man must be lived in the midst of organized iniquity, in one form or another, there is but one recourse, and men, who are men, must stand with the Christ and "stick to God in stable trust," for

> "He always wins who sides with God;
> For him no chance is lost."

If men doubt this, let them recall what Queen Elizabeth told the merchant to whom she had given an important commission. The merchant objected: "What will become of my business if I undertake this?" "You attend to my business," said the majestic monarch, "and I will take charge of your affairs." My dear reader, that will be your good fortune if you put first things *first;* namely, "every word that proceedeth out of the mouth of God."

If men will but shut out of their ears the incessant clatter, the rumbling grind, the shrieking voices of the world's all-absorbing interests, they will hear another voice, a voice exactly meant to guide them out of earth's shams into all truth; out of sin into righteousness; out of doom into bliss; out of the parched desert into God's green pastures, and beside the still waters of His peace. It is the voice of the Good Shepherd, who calls all His sheep by name, and who said: "My sheep hear my voice, and I know them, and they follow Me; and I give unto them eternal life; and they shall never perish, neither shall any man pluck them out of my hand." As of yore, the voice of Jesus sounds o'er land and sea: "Whosoever drinketh of this water shall thirst again; but whosoever drinketh of the water that I shall give him shall never thirst." Let men hear that voice. Do you hear it?

> "O, may I join the choir invisible
> Of those immortal dead, who live again
> In minds made better by their presence; live
> In pulses stirred to generosity,
> In deeds of daring rectitude, in scorn
> For miserable aims that end with self,
> In thoughts sublime that pierce the night like stars.
> And with their mild persistence urge men's search
> To vaster issues."